CARE INSTRUCTIONS

poems by

Tanya Sangpun Thamkruphat

Finishing Line Press
Georgetown, Kentucky

CARE INSTRUCTIONS

Copyright © 2024 by Tanya Sangpun Thamkruphat
ISBN 979-8-88838-500-5 First Edition
All rights reserved under International and Pan-American Copyright Conventions. No part of this book may be reproduced in any manner whatsoever without written permission from the publisher, except in the case of brief quotations embodied in critical articles and reviews.

ACKNOWLEDGMENTS

Much love, hugs, high fives, and eternal thanks to my family, friends, cats (RIP Diana The Huntress), strangers, acquaintances, coworkers, and everyone else in between who showed up for me during my darkest timeline. These poems are for you.

Publisher: Leah Huete de Maines
Editor: Christen Kincaid
Cover Art: Magda Ehlers via pexels.com
Author Photo: Tanya Sangpun Thamkruphat
Cover Design: Elizabeth Maines McCleavy

Order online: www.finishinglinepress.com
also available on amazon.com

Author inquiries and mail orders:
Finishing Line Press
PO Box 1626
Georgetown, Kentucky 40324
USA

Contents

The Relay Race 1

Home, Sweet, Home. 2

Hello, Universe... 3

The Mind's Eye 4

Keep Fighting 5

The Light 6

Unwanted Guests 7

Guilty Pleasure 8

Pennies and Nickels 9

Adventure Awaits 10

Care Instructions 11

Quiet Zone 12

The Dead is Now Living 13

Cereal 14

Ocean of Changes 15

Do Not Copy and Paste 16

Parallel Universes 17

The Epic Farewell Tour 18

Low Sodium, Low Fat, Guilt-Free Life 19

Only Holier Than Thyself 20

The Relay Race

Sometimes, life feels like you're in a relay race,
while running with a boulder,
with the expectation to perform well
with little guidance
and no practice.
Don't let self-doubt, anxiety, and peers bully you.
Struggles and failures are inevitable,
but, in your own time,
your growth and victories will be, too.

Home, Sweet, Home

In life, you make choices that you defend
with every breath,
diving into the unknown.
You hope that you swiftly swim
or freely float,
hardly unscathed.
Though, sometimes you slowly drown
from wrong choices,
with self-punishment clamping and tugging and nagging.
But, do not let it.
Allow the learned lessons to remind you
that there are many parts of the vast ocean
sweetly singing for you to call home.

Hello, Universe

When the world wasn't receptive of my voice,
I turned to the universe.
I greeted it,
closed my eyes,
inhaled,
exhaled,
and deeply rooted myself
in a seated conversation with it.
There were days I whispered to the universe,
carrying heavy rain and thunder clouds in my heart.
Other days I sang,
with a grating voice,
but with a grateful heart, to it.
The universe has been a great confidant.
It holds no judgment when others do.
Instead, it holds space for
my thoughts,
my emotions,
and, most importantly,
me.

The Mind's Eye

Your mind's eye is powerful,
recollecting memories
for which you desire and ache,
sometimes for too many suns and moons.
However, it is a visionary,
imagining a future,
which you, the master,
architect what can be.
Be kind to yourself.
The future belongs to you.

Keep Fighting

Your fists clench into punching gloves,
unprepared to fight the sleepless nights.
Your body aches from the unrelenting anxiety.
Your breath shortens as panic manhandles you.
These fights are tough, but so are you.
You will have losses.
And, you will have wins.
But, no matter what, you are a champion.
No one can take the fighter out of you.

The Light

The light we seek has been touted
as radiant and welcoming.
However, sometimes, the light is dim,
veiled by gray skies.
Sometimes, it is uninviting,
providing minimal comfort.
Or, sometimes, it is not easily found,
hidden among storms.
But, do not rush to disappointment.
The light exists differently, from day to day.
Yet, it does not make it less astounding.

Unwanted Guests

Your emotions can unexpectedly arrive,
insistent about unpacking their heavy baggage.
While you hesitate to allow them in,
they barge in, trampling your day.
They usually overstay their welcome,
but you don't know how to ask them to leave.
So, you wallow in discomfort while
you mull over what to do with them.
Do you connect with them?
Do you throw them out?
The answer is
to do what is best
for you and your mental health.

Guilty Pleasure

The feast of everyone's hearty joys feed my heart.
I indulge in their happiness,
quickly consuming it
while anticipating more.
But, as my heart rapidly approaches fullness,
I slow down
to heave deep, satisfying sighs,
to ensure there is ample space,
for a guilty
pleasure,
my happiness.

Pennies and Nickels

If I was offered a penny for my thoughts,
if I offered my two cents,
and if I had a nickel
for every poem I wrote
I would not be poor or rich.
I would have change,
to give and to take,
loudly jangling
for the world to hear
my freedom
of expression.

Adventure Awaits

Stories, from life and fiction,
sow the seeds of inspiration within us.
From pleasure and pain, we birth newborn dreams.
Our dreams are nurtured, fed, and protected.
We watch them sprout into adolescent goals,
changing through trial and error.
Soon enough, they mature into plans,
ready for adventures.

Care Instructions

When your mind is stained
with doubt, fear, and worry,
wash it in self-love
on a gentle cycle of
kind words,
loving thoughts,
and unconditional care.
Tumble dry low-key
until you're ready to face another day.

Quiet Zone

The quiet zone is unique to everyone.
It is carved from needing to recharge.
Here you only receive signals
from your telling body and mind.
Here you roam with your feelings and thoughts.
Create a stable connection with yourself.
It doesn't need to be executed
lightning fast or at high speeds.
Remove all unnecessary data.
Once recharged, you'll operate with fewer glitches,
and feeling 100%.

The Dead is Now Living

Transform your past experiences
into a thriving living.

Cereal

Life is a mixed container of sugary and bland cereals.
Some days your bowl is filled more with the sugary kind.
If you're lucky, you get the surprise prize.
Other days your bowl is filled more with the bland kind,
barely tasting any sweetness.
And, on rare days, you don't have to eat cereal.
Instead, you are treated to gorge on a heavenly buffet.

Ocean of Change

I'm trying to slowly immerse myself in the ocean of changes because anxiety is hella real, and I'm not a strong swimmer.

But, I'm going to continue swimming.

Do Not Copy and Paste

You cannot copy and paste love
from other documented relationships.
You cannot expect the same format
to work for you as it has for others.
Each love is stylistically unique.
Each love does not contain the same content as the next.
Remember to write your own love.

Parallel Universes

Our worlds are morphing,
they are slipping through our fingers,
as we try to grasp it
with fluid emotions,
as we try to hold it together with love, laughs, and lifelines.
We live in the same world,
but in parallel universes.

As much as we long for normalcy,
we cannot return to it.
It is not healthy and safe for any of us.
We must let it go like letting go of bad love,
to leave behind the toxicity,
to be in a better space,
and have time to heal.
It is time to establish a new world,
the same world,
in the same universe,
together.

The Epic Farewell Tour

We don't get to choose
when we die
or how we die,
but we can decide,
before our final day,
how we will be
celebrated,
mourned,
respected,
cherished,
or remembered
at death.
That is a privilege
that other species do not have.
That is a power
we should embrace.
Death is terrifying,
but think of it this way.
Death is our epic farewell tour
that unites our fans
to cry about ,
talk about ,
laugh about,
and uninhibitedly sing
both our popular and obscure songs.

Low Sodium, Low Fat, Guilt-Free Life

Eliminate the salty, junk people in your life.
Increase your intake of wholesome ones.
Side effects include, but are not limited to,
sleeping well,
reduced stress,
and gaining a healthy support system.
Getting vitamins C(at) and D(og) are recommended.
Treat your troubled thoughts to prevent infections.
Meditate, meditate, meditate.
Exercise your right to live your life.
Hydrate so you don't become a thirsty person.
And, don't forget to eat your fruits and vegetables.

Only Holier Than Thyself

You venture to a faraway place
where they say you would find peace,
nestled deep within the bosom of the earth.
They say there exists your salvation.
When you arrive
there is nothing
but Mother Nature
and yourself.
You cry because you traveled so far.
You searched until
you became weathered.
Yet, you never stopped
to think for a moment
that perhaps you are
your own salvation.

Tanya Sangpun Thamkruphat is a Thai-Vietnamese American poet and essayist. Her writing is focused on advocating for an open dialogue about mental health, body image, identity, culture and heritage, and relationships, especially in relation to the diaspora experience. In her writing, she mainly writes slice-of-life stories set against a surrealist backdrop because she believes that life is bizarre but our reactions and emotions to the strange and unexpected are utterly relatable.

Tanya is the author of the poetry chapbooks, *Em(body)ment of Wonder* (Raine Poetry Publishing, 2021) and *It Wasn't a Dream* (Fahmidan Publishing & Co., 2022). Her writing appears in *The Orange County Register, Button Poetry, Honey Literary, The Cincinnati Review, San Diego Poetry Annual, 2022-2023, Midway Journal, Rio Grande Review, West Trestle Review*, and elsewhere. She's also a 2023 Kenyon Review alum.

Tanya lives with her partner and feline overlord in Southern California. You can follow her on Twitter (@madamewritelyso) and on Instagram (@madamewritelyso).

www.ingramcontent.com/pod-product-compliance
Lightning Source LLC
Chambersburg PA
CBHW030053100426
42734CB00038B/1537